D0875880

Callie

Callie

Dave Sargent

Ozark Publishing, Inc.
P.O. Box 228
Prairie Grove, AR 72753

Library of Congress Cataloging-in-Publication Data

Sargent, Dave, 1941-
    Callie / Dave Sargent .
       p. cm.
    Summary: A biography of the author's
grandmother, which follows her hard life as she
raised fourteen children mostly on her own while
her husband was away working for the Texas
Rangers or fighting in several wars.
    ISBN 1-56763-014-6 (cloth : alk. paper).
— ISBN 1-56763-002-2(paper : alk. paper)
    1. Nicholson, Callie Many Waters Cox,
1869-1956—Juvenile literature. 2. Texas—
Biography—Juvenile literature. 3. Women—
Texas—Biography—Juvenile literature.   [1.
Nicholson, Callie Many Waters Cox, 1869-1956.
2. Family life—Texas. 3. Texas—Biography. 4.
Women—Biography.] 1. Title.
CT275.N666S27   1996
976.4'06'092—dc20
[B]

                      96-33905
                         CIP
                          AC

Printed in the United States of America

Inspired by

Irene's desire for her children, grand-children, great-grandchildren, and future generations to know something of their heritage, and of Callie.

Dedicated to

Irene, Callie's only living child.

Foreword

The master reared back from the table and lit his cigar. He said, "Callie, you'll be leaving tomorrow. I've given you to a Texas Ranger to marry, so I guess you'll be going to Texas."

Callie, only twelve, was stunned by the master's words. She was scared, but excited. Anything would be better than living on a cotton plantation in near-slavery conditions.

Callie and the Texas Ranger began a life together that brought both happiness and sadness, and sometimes heartbreak to Callie.

Alone most of the time, she knew few pleasures in life, but she learned to love. Over the years, she gave birth to seventeen children.

This is the story of her never-ending struggle of caring for her family and surviving under sometimes heart-breaking conditions.

Contents

Callie

One

Little Dove

It was a warm spring day in 1869 when Little Dove gave birth to a baby girl. Little Dove was a full-blood Cherokee Indian, just barely fourteen years old. Her husband, George Cox, was a blond-headed, blue-eyed Irishman.

George met Little Dove in an Indian village in Oklahoma where he was trading with the Indians. It was late fall, 1867. He was twenty-five. She was twelve.

When George saw Little Dove for the first time, she was running through the village, and even though she was only twelve, she was in full bloom. For George, it was love at first sight. He asked the chief if he would speak to the father of Little Dove for him, and after a lot of dickering back and forth, George finally struck a deal with her father. He traded two horses, three bottles of whiskey, four blankets, and a mirror for her.

George and Little Dove were married in the village under Indian law, and that night they left the camp and headed southeast to begin their lives together.

They traveled for three days, taking turns riding the only horse they had, before reaching George's small one-room cabin which he had built in the foothills of the Ouachita Mountains. They spent the winter there, and George trapped beaver and raccoons.

George had traded with the Indians since the end of the Civil War. He had joined the Confederate Army as soon as the war broke out. He managed to survive several fierce battles without a scratch, only to go home to Missouri to find that his family had been massacred by raiders and the family home burned. With nothing left in Missouri, he had headed for the Oklahoma Territory and had started trading with the Indians.

George had learned much of the Cherokee language, and if he couldn't speak certain words, he used sign language.

George and Little Dove spent many hours that winter sitting in front of the fireplace teaching each other their native tongue. By spring, each of them could converse in either language.

That spring when the dogwoods opened their buds and displayed their snow-white pedals, signifying the beginning of another growing season, George loaded up his winter catch of pelts and headed for Fort Smith, Arkansas, to trade them for supplies and ammunition. He left Little Dove at the cabin and told her that he would return before the next full moon, which would be in about ten days.

When he got back from Fort Smith,

he had a pack horse loaded with flour, corn, sugar, beans, coffee, and salt. Now they had all they would need to live in luxury. It would be a year before he would make another trip to town.

Two

Many Waters

Summer was a time for preparing for winter. George and Little Dove dried much meat during the hot part of summer, in preparation for the coming winter. That fall, after the first frost, Little Dove told George that she was going to have a baby and that it would be born in the spring.

For the first time, they went back to the village to see her family, and although they didn't know it, it would also be the last.

After returning to their cabin, they spent the winter making plans for the future and their lives together.

In the spring when their daughter was born, she was named Many Waters by her mother, and was named Callie Cox by her father.

Callie had jet-black hair like her mother, yet it was as fine as silk, like George's. Her eyes were bright blue, and her skin was a pale white. Many Waters was a beautiful baby.

George and Little Dove decided to go to Texas and start a ranch, but they would wait until Callie was a year old before leaving. That would give George time to get enough pelts to trade for a wagon.

That winter he worked hard to get as many pelts as he could. It was a long, hard winter, and when the weather finally broke in early March, he packed up all his pelts and headed for Fort Smith. Since it took both horses to carry all the pelts, he had to walk and lead them.

The pelts were worth more that year than they had been in the past, so he was able to get a covered wagon and enough supplies to last for a good spell. He even had a few dollars left. He went back to the cabin and waited until the rainy season was over. They then loaded up and headed for Texas.

They had traveled for five weeks when they found a beautiful, fertile valley which stretched for miles. It was flat and had a stream flowing gently through the middle of it. To the east were rolling hills with lots of good timber.

George and Little Dove made camp on a hill overlooking the valley and decided that this was where they would build their home. They laid claim to the hill and the valley below. They had settled just north of a place called Fort Worth.

George, wanting to be proud of the home they were building, set in cutting timber from the hill. He hewed the logs with great care.

It was late spring, 1871, before the house was finished. George had built a two-story log house facing the west, overlooking the lush green valley below. The house had three rooms downstairs and two rooms upstairs, with a full length porch across the front and another across the back. He had built a large fireplace on the north end.

With the house now complete, George decided to dig a well near the house. They had been carrying water from the stream, which was more than a quarter of a mile away.

The summer passed as George and Little Dove dug the well. George would dig and put the rocks and dirt in an oaken bucket, and Little Dove would hoist it out of the well, dump it, and lower it down again.

After digging seventeen feet, George broke into slate. Two feet into the slate, as he brought down the pick with all the force he could muster, crystal clear, cold, sweet water bubbled up. It had taken four months to dig the well.

Callie was now two and a half years old, and Little Dove was with child again. Settlers were moving in all around now. It seemed like new ones were arriving every day.

Even with all the neighbors, George and Little Dove were loners. Because Little Dove was Indian, she wasn't accepted.

With the well now dug, George decided to line it with rocks to keep it from caving in. Using a sled he had made, he hauled rocks to the well, then piled them around the top of it. He would drop a few down in the well, then climb down inside and stack those rocks around the wall of the well. This process was repeated over and over.

George had built the wall to a height of six feet, when all of a sudden, the rim of the well gave way. A large rock fell into the well striking him on the head, killing him.

Little Dove was left alone, six months with child, and with Callie only two and a half years old.

Shortly before Little Dove was due to give birth, the doctor from Fort Worth stopped by to see her. He talked her into going home with him so that she could stay with him and his wife until her baby was born.

One month after moving in with the doctor and his wife, Little Dove, now sixteen, gave birth to a baby boy. He had coarse black hair, a dark complexion, and deep brown eyes. He looked like a full-blood Indian, not at all like Callie. Little Dove called him Edward Cox, the name George had chosen before he died.

Shortly after giving birth, Little Dove began running a high fever. Three days later, she died. Now, Callie and her newborn brother, Edward, had no one.

The doctor and his wife were

newlyweds and had no children, so they decided to keep the two kids for awhile. But, when the doctor's wife gave birth to a boy a year later, Callie and Edward were no longer welcome.

The young doctor, whose name was not remembered, found a home for Callie on a cotton plantation in Louisiana. The fate of Edward Cox, to this day, is unknown. Callie never heard his name again.

Three

The Little House Girl

Now, at the age of five, Callie found herself living in a mansion, but living there as a slave. She was the house girl for the mistress of the house, responding to her every beck and call. She was never allowed schooling. She never learned to read or write. She never even learned to write her own name.

Slavery had been abolished, but the blacks who lived on the plantation lived as they had done all their lives. Even though they were free, they couldn't leave because they had no place to go and had no way to survive. Callie was living like the blacks, where the only pay they got was the food they ate and the beds they slept in.

Once, when Callie was five, the master of the house called her in and said, "Fetch my riding boots, girl."

"I don't feel good," Callie replied.

She was lashed across the back with a cat-o'-nine-tails which brought welts and drew blood. From that point on, Callie was a good little house girl. No matter how sick she was, she always did whatever she was told to do.

In 1877, when Callie was eight years old, the master of the house got up earlier than usual one morning, and, as he looked down from his two-story window, he saw a black man slipping out of the smokehouse with something tucked under his shirt. The master hurried downstairs and got his pistol, then slipped out the back door. He followed the black man to his shanty and walked in just as the black man pulled a cut of ham from under his shirt. The black man had young children, too young to work in the fields, and because they were too young to work, they were not given a ration of food. There was not enough food in the shanty for that size family to survive. The black man had stolen a piece of ham so that his kids would not go hungry.

The master brought him at gunpoint to the front of the mansion and lashed him to a sycamore tree. Callie remembered that it was the hot part of summer and the man was left there all that day without water. Then, just before sundown, all the field hands were forced to gather on the front lawn, and the household was forced to watch from the veranda. The master walked up to the black man and grabbed him by the shirt collar. He ripped the shirt from his body, then, with the cat-o'-nine-tails, lashed the man across the back. The cat of nine tails lashed out, again and again. And finally, the black man's body relaxed and hung limp.

Several times, Callie tried to look away, but the mistress would turn her face back toward the scene and say, "You watch this, girl, and remember what you see, because if you get out of line or steal anything, the same thing will happen to you."

The master didn't stop lashing the man with the cat-o'-nine-tails until the man was dead. He then turned and faced the field hands and said, as his eyes swept over them and the servants on the veranda, "Any man caught stealing will get the same punishment."

Callie said later that she remembered the man's body staying tied to the tree all that night and all the next day, and then, finally, just before sundown, it was cut loose and thrown into the river.

For several months, Callie would wake up in the middle of the night, scared to death. She was afraid to eat scraps from the table. She ate only what was put on her plate and was afraid to ask for more. That experience burned deep in her heart. And she knew that if she ever lost her memory, that would surely be the last thing she would ever forget.

In the spring of 1881, Callie was twelve years old, and, like her mother, she had developed and matured young. It was a hot summer day, getting on toward mid-afternoon, when a neighbor rode up, got off his horse, and tied it to the hitching post. He walked up the steps to the veranda and sat down in the porch swing and started talking to the master. The master was laid back in his rocking chair with his feet propped up on the porch rail. He puffed on a cigar, stopping only long enough to sip on his brandy.

Callie heard the neighbor say, "There's going to be a hanging tomorrow. Everyone for miles around is going to be there. It's going to take place at two o'clock."

The next morning, the day of the hanging, everyone was up early fixing fried chicken and all the trimmings for a grand picnic. The master was taking the mistress and the entire household staff to the hanging party.

It was late morning by the time everything was ready. Two of the field hands led the team and carriage to the front of the mansion, went back for the horses and wagon and brought them to the front, then stood patiently waiting.

The carriage was hitched to two solid-black high-spirited mares. They were groomed to perfection. Their coats glistened and seemed to sparkle, reflecting the sun's rays like a mirror. The wagon was pulled by a matching pair of Clydesdale geldings. The master was known for his beautiful well-matched teams, but the black mares were the pride of the plantation.

The household staff, which consisted of Callie, a young black boy called Billy, and four women older than Callie, had an extra change of clothes which they wore only when the master was entertaining guests. Today the master wanted to show off at the hanging party and had everyone dress in his very best.

The master and the mistress climbed into the carriage; the household staff loaded the picnic supplies and themselves in the open wagon; and they headed toward town.

The carriage was driven by a well-dressed middle-age black man. He took care of the stable and was the only one allowed to drive the carriage. With the exception of the master, this black man was the best-dressed man on the plantation.

Four

The Hanging

The ride to town took almost an hour. As the carriage pulled onto the town square, the gallows came into view. It had been erected right in the middle of the square. There was already a crowd there of around two hundred people. They had come from miles around to have a good time and watch a man being executed by hanging.

They went half-way around the square before finding a place to pull up. As soon as the wagon stopped, the household got busy setting up the picnic. They placed two barrels on the red brick walk which circled the square. Then they placed a slab-wood table top on the barrels and covered it with a red-and- white checked gingham tablecloth. Then they laid out a feast that would satiate the hunger of any man.

Everyone there was having a picnic. Some had set up tables, while others were using their wagons and buckboards. Some had just spread their food on a cloth on the ground.

After the picnic was over, the left-overs were put away, and the area was made tidy. The household staff was told that they could stroll around town until after the hanging was over.

Callie was pretty much a loner, so, as Billy and the other girls made their way through the crowd, Callie looked at the gallows. Awed by what was about to happen, she felt uneasy. She noticed a tall, medium-built stranger standing next to the marshal. He appeared to be staring at her. She turned away and started moving slowly around the square. Every time she glanced toward the gallows, she caught the stranger looking at her.

Callie, more nervous than ever about the stranger's continuous stare, made her way back to the security of the master's presence. The stranger seemed to be slowly moving closer to where Callie was standing. She was standing with her head down, but she glanced up from time to time to watch his slow, but sure approach. As she glanced up, she caught a glimpse of a star on his shirt that was partially hidden by his brown leather vest. He was a young man who looked to be twenty or so. His hair was a sandy brown, and his eyes were a faded blue. He was well groomed and clean shaven. His Texas hat was a dark brown, matching his vest and boots. Callie noted his gun belt with two holsters, each containing a pearl-handled Colt .45. The gun belt matched his hat, boots, and vest. His spurs sparkled of shiny silver. His stare was broken when the marshal called out, "Ed!" He turned and walked toward the gallows.

Callie herself was a beautiful young girl. Though only twelve, she looked seventeen. She had jet-black hair, heavy black eyebrows, and long black eyelashes. Her eyes were a bright blue, standing out against her light complexion. Standing five feet one, she was truly a beautiful young girl.

After seeing the stranger's star, Callie felt more at ease, knowing he was a lawman. She now made eye contact with him from time to time, displaying a little curiosity about his long, steady looks.

Just before the hanging was scheduled to take place, Callie glanced up to see the stranger walking straight toward her. She turned and hurried through the anxiously awaiting crowd to her master's side. He had wandered away while she was concentrating on the stranger. Once she was safe beside her master, she turned to see the man with the star still making his way through the crowd, following her.

Callie stepped behind the master as the stranger stopped directly in front of him and said, "Howdy, mister. My name's Ed, Ed Nicholson. I've been seeing a young black-haired girl with you. Would she be yours?"

"She would," the master retorted.

"Is she spoken for?" the stranger asked.

"No. Why?" asked the master.

The stranger said, "I'd like to talk to you," and motioned for the master to walk across the street with him. They walked away together. After a few minutes, they returned to where Callie was nervously waiting. The stranger turned toward the gallows, and, as he walked away, he said to the master, "I'll see you after the hanging's over."

The street around the square was now

so filled with people that it was hard for Callie to even move. She watched as the marshal and the stranger made their way through the crowd and across the street toward the jail. Once they were inside, the crowd grew silent. It was like the still before the storm. Callie couldn't hear a sound.

Then, the door to the jail opened and out stepped a man in shackles and chains. Suddenly, the crowd roared! They could be heard for miles. The marshal was carrying a shotgun and every few steps, he would nudge the convicted man in the back with the gun, forcing him closer to the gallows.

As they approached the gallows, the noise started to lull, and, as they started up the stairs, once again, total silence fell upon the crowd.

The condemned man slowly made his way up the steps, never taking his eyes off the rope that would control his destiny. The crowd was silent as the doomed man stepped onto the trap door and the marshal placed the noose around his neck. The marshal stood on one side and the stranger, called Ed Nicholson, stood on the other.

After what seemed to be an eternity, the church bell started to ring. At the first sound of the bell, the trapdoor on the gallows dropped open, and a low, muffled roar came from the crowd. The hanging was over.

The crowd started to break up. The master sent the household staff back to the plantation. He and the mistress remained in town. As the wagon left the square, Callie glanced up to see the stranger raise his hand to wave to her. She turned away, ignoring the gesture.

That night when the call for supper was made, the master ordered Callie to sit at the table with him and the mistress. None of the household had ever sat at the master's table before.

As Callie sat down, she didn't know what to think or what to expect. She sat there waiting. The mistress said, "You'd better eat, girl. It's a long time until morning."

Callie picked at her food, still not knowing why she had been ordered to the table.

After supper, the table was cleared and the master reared back and lit his cigar, then said, "Callie, you'll be leaving tomorrow. I have given you to Ed Nicholson to marry. He's coming tomorrow morning to pick you up. He's a Texas Ranger, so he'll be taking you to Texas with him."

That night Callie couldn't sleep. She was torn between fear and anticipation. She wanted to get out from under the cruel ruling hand of the master, and yet, she feared the uncertain fate that lay ahead.

It was mid-morning when the stranger rode up. He was riding a sorrel and leading a bay. Callie was upstairs with her face pressed against the window. As he stepped down and tied the horses to the hitching post, the mistress walked up behind Callie and called her name. Callie turned quickly, her face red from having been caught staring down at the man.

The mistress handed Callie a valise and said, "Hurry! Pack your belongings."

The chore of packing took only a minute. Callie's "belongings" were two dresses plus what she was wearing. She was ordered to the veranda where the stranger awaited her.

As Callie walked out the front door, the stranger was standing next to the steps. He removed his hat, stuck out his hand, and said, "Callie, my name is Elischa George Nicholson, but my friends call me Ed."

Callie reached out and shook his hand. He took her valise and helped her on the horse he had brought for her, then climbed on his own horse and they rode off, heading west toward Texas.

As they topped a small hill, Callie stopped and looked back for a long time, vowing to herself to never forget the pain and suffering she had endured over the last seven years. She knew that no matter what lay ahead, it had to be better than the past.

She turned and rode down the hill, out of sight of the plantation, with a smile on her face for the first time ever. She never looked back again.

Five

A Wedding under the Stars

Callie and Ed rode west until late in the afternoon. When they came to a small creek, Ed stopped and said, "We'll make camp here for the night." He located a gravel bar next to a large water hole and that's where they set up camp.

Ed left Callie sitting on the gravel bar while he staked out the horses and hunted for some game. He was gone for about a half hour before returning with two nice rabbits. He cooked them over an open fire in an atmosphere that was quiet and peaceful.

As darkness started to settle in, Ed spread out his bedroll on the gravel bar. He and Callie lay there facing each other with the flickering of the low flames setting their faces aglow.

Ed took Callie's hands in his and gently squeezed them as he said, "Callie, you are the most beautiful girl I've ever seen. I vow to you here and now that I will never hurt you. I'll treat you like a princess, and I'll love you with all my heart."

Callie said, "I don't know what it is to love, but I will learn, and I will always be by your side."

And with those vows in their minds and in their hearts, under the watchful eyes of God, they were married.

The next morning, they continued on toward Austin, where the Texas Rangers were headquartered. Ed had taken his prisoner to Louisiana to be hanged, and he was supposed to report back as quickly as possible. The trip would take six days. They spent that time telling each other about their lives.

When Ed heard Callie's story, he

was saddened. It was only then that he learned her age, but at this point, age didn't matter. By the end of the six days, they had established a bond that could never be broken.

Ed told Callie that he had been born and raised on a plantation owned by his father in Kentucky. He was well schooled. At the age of twelve he had been sent to a seminary. His mother wanted him to be a minister. After a year at the seminary he ran away, but his family found him and took him back to the plantation where he spent the next year working in the fields alongside the field hands.

Ed's father had felt that if Ed had to work like most people, he would learn to appreciate the finer things in life.

After a year of working in the fields, Ed was sent back to the seminary. He stayed for one year before running away again. It wasn't the kind of life he wanted.

Ed's older brother, John, was sent to find Ed to tell him that he had been disinherited and that he was never to come back to the plantation. It was then that Ed had decided to go to Texas.

When Ed had arrived in Austin, he had tried to join the Texas Rangers, but was told that he was too young. He got a job in a blacksmith shop where he worked until he was eighteen. At age eighteen, he was allowed to join the Texas Rangers. Being a ranger became his life, and he was good at it.

After six days, Ed and Callie reached Austin. Ed had a two-room shack about two miles from town and that was where they would live. After settling in, he went into town to check in and pick up some supplies. While he was gone, Callie cleaned the shack, scrubbing it until even the floors were as shiny as glass.

When Ed got back, he was pleased with how she had been able, in such a short time, to make the shack look like a real home. Because she was a house girl, Callie had never learned to cook. Her duties had been those of washing dishes, washing clothes, making beds, and the general cleaning of the house. Ed wasn't worried when Callie told him that she didn't know how to cook, that she had never been allowed to learn. He simply said, "Don't worry, Callie. You'll have plenty of time to learn."

One day they ran out of the coffee that Ed had parched and ground, so he went to the corner of the room where extra supplies were stored and picked up a large sack of coffee beans. He said, "Callie, you'll need to parch these while I go into town for some things." He then proceeded to explain exactly how it was done.

Ed left for town, and Callie got a fire going in the kitchen stove. She put the coffee beans in a pan and set it in the oven. She hadn't given the stove enough time to heat up, so the beans wouldn't parch. She checked them several times at first, and since the beans weren't even hot, she decided it would probably take all day, so she didn't open the oven again until late that afternoon. She was going in and out, working in the yard, such as it was, and suddenly, remembering the coffee beans, she rushed into the house and pulled the oven door open. The coffee beans were burned to a dark brown powder!

Callie was scared! This was the first thing she had done by herself, and she had messed it up. She had ruined the coffee beans. Afraid that Ed would be angry, and worried about what he might do, she took the burned beans, ran out the door, and buried them under a rock.

That evening when Ed rode up, he could smell coffee from a distance. As he entered the house, the smell was much stronger. He said, "Callie, put on a pot of coffee, and we'll have a cup."

Callie took a deep breath, and, with a low voice, said, "I forgot to parch the beans."

Ed knew by the smell that she had attempted to do what he had asked, so he just grinned and put his arm around her. He said, "Let's parch some together." Nothing else was ever said about it.

About a month had gone by since the coffee-parching incident. Ed had made bread several times, with Callie watching everything he did. They had even made it together a few times. One day she decided to impress him by making it on her own. When Ed headed for town, she hurriedly set the ingredients on the table and started making bread.

It was a cool, cloudy day, and the temperature was much cooler than normal. Callie didn't put in enough yeast, plus, the weather was cool; and the yeast, which makes bread rise, needed to be warm in order for it to work, so the bread wouldn't rise.

Finally, by late afternoon Callie decided the bread was ruined, so she buried it out in front of the house, just under the surface of the ground.

Ed didn't go to town the next day. He and Callie worked all day, just fixing things up around the house. It was a nice warm day, and late that afternoon they went outside to choose a place to plant a fall garden. They were going to plant some tulips and some fast-growing vegetables. As they passed the place where Callie had buried the bread, Ed noticed a large bulge in the ground. Thinking it was a varmint that had burrowed under the surface, he stomped it with the heel of his boot. His boot went to the bottom of the hole and the bread bulged up all around it. He gasped and pulled his foot out of the hole, then dug up the bread.

Callie watched, not saying a word. Ed looked the bread over good and asked, "Callie, do you know what this is?"

Callie told Ed what she had done and all he said, was, "Next time, don't bury it so soon. This bread wasn't as dead as you thought." They both had a good laugh, but the dead-bread episode was never forgotten. It was laughed about many times over the years.

There were times when Ed would be gone for a week or two at a time when he was sent out to catch someone who had broken the law. Callie had just turned thirteen and was about four-months pregnant when Ed stopped by the house to pick up his bedroll and a few supplies. He hugged Callie and said, "I'm going on a manhunt, and I may be gone for awhile, but don't worry. I'll be back as soon as I can." He gave Callie what money he had, then headed out for parts unknown.

Ed had been gone for nearly two months before Callie heard any news of him. Then, one day a ranger stopped by. He said, "We've been in touch with Ed.

He wants you to take the train to Fort Worth and meet him there. There's been a lot of trouble in Fort Worth, and he's being transferred there."

Callie packed her things and Ed's things. She sold the extra horse, then caught the train to Fort Worth.

Just before the train got to Dallas, which was still a good ways from Fort Worth, she went into labor. She was six-months pregnant and only thirteen years old. By the time the train stopped in Dallas, she had passed out. She was unconscious and had to be carried from the train. She was taken to the boarding house, and the doctor was notified.

When the doctor arrived, Callie was awake and hysterical. The baby was stillborn. It was a little boy. Callie now lay on the bed, unconscious. Ed, in Fort Worth, was unaware of the tragedy.

It was two days before Callie came to, and it was another three days before she even realized that she was no longer carrying the baby.

News got to Ed about a week later. As soon as he got word, he went to Dallas to be with her. By the time he got there, Callie was feeling much better. He stayed with her for a few days, then they took the train to Fort Worth.

Ed had made a deal for a small place just out of town, and he took Callie there. He didn't like being around people, even though his job as a ranger forced him to. When he wasn't working, he wanted to be alone. Except now there was Callie, but Ed thought of her as a part of himself.

As time passed, the bond between Ed and Callie grew stronger. Callie's love for Ed was heightened by her respect and admiration for him. Just as he had vowed when they married themselves before God, under the stars, he treated her with love and respect. Now, for the first time since her mother, Little Dove, died, Callie knew real love.

Six

The Cotton Field

There was lots of trouble in Fort Worth now. It was full of gunfighters and drifters. Someone was getting killed just every few days.

Ed was now spending more time tracking down murderers and robbers than he was spending at home. He was good at what he did. He loved being a Texas Ranger, and he was fast with a gun. Those were the things that contributed to his success. And besides being well educated, he had a lot of common sense.

Callie was pregnant again, about eight months along, when Ed took off to track down a man who had robbed the Wells Fargo Office. Ed's chase took him all the way to El Paso before he caught his man, and then, it ended in a shoot-out. It was three months before he made it back home.

When Ed walked into the house, he found that Callie had given birth to another boy, and it had been stillborn, too, just like the first. Callie had turned fourteen a few months before the baby was born. Both Ed and Callie were saddened by their loss, but they knew there would be other children.

It had been a little over a year since their second son had been stillborn when Callie told Ed that she was pregnant again. They were still living just outside Fort Worth. Callie was now fifteen, and her beauty was the envy of all women.

Shortly after turning sixteen, Callie gave birth to another boy, but it, too, was stillborn. They became very concerned now, wondering if they would ever be able to have a family.

Six months later, Callie was with

child again. It was about that time that Ed was transferred to Waco, where he again found a small place just outside of town.

Just before Callie was to give birth, Ed headed out across the great open plains of Texas to track down a man wanted for murder. While he was gone, Callie gave birth to another boy. This one survived. Callie was barely seventeen when this baby was born. When Ed got home, he was a proud man. They named the baby John.

A year later, Callie gave birth to another boy. He was named Leo. Then, at age twenty, their first girl was born and was named Ethyl.

Train robbing had become the profession of a lot of men. They found trains to be easy prey. Wells Fargo offered Ed a job tracking down train robbers. It was a job that would keep him away for as long as a year or more at a time, and it seemed to Callie that he was only home just long enough to move her to a new place, make her pregnant, and see the latest addition to the family.

Over the years, Callie gave birth to seventeen children, and Ed was never there when one was born.

By the time Callie was twenty-one years old, she had given birth to seven babies. Four were living, and ranged from newborn to four years old.

When Ed would leave, he'd always give Callie some money, but it was never enough. The money always ran out a few months after he left and Callie was forced to move into town with the kids and take in washing, ironing, and sewing, in order to buy food for herself and the kids.

Each time Ed came home, he'd move Callie and the children to a new town, make her pregnant, and then take off on another manhunt, as he called it. He never wanted Callie living in town. He always moved her to a place a few miles out of town. It was only after the money ran out that she would move to town so she could work and make enough money for food.

Callie never had a way to travel. Many times, her neighbors would stop by and tell her that if she would give them a list, they would pick up some supplies for her and the kids, but more often than not, Callie, with child, would carry the youngest one, while the older ones walked alongside, all the way to town and buy what supplies they could tote back. Even the two-and three-year-old kids would carry what they could.

Callie's eighth child was another girl. They named her Callie. Baby Callie lived only a couple of days.

Their ninth child was a boy and Callie named him George, but when Ed came home again, he said, "He can keep the name George, but I'll always call him Dick."

Callie was now twenty-three, and Ed left again. This time he was tracking down two men who had robbed a Wells Fargo Office and killed the attendant. Six months had passed without any word from or about Ed. It took a lot to feed five kids, and with the money and all their supplies gone, Callie moved to town where she did the only things she knew how to do: washing, ironing, and sewing.

Callie couldn't get enough work to make enough money to care for the kids. A lot of cotton was being grown in Texas at that time, so she started working in the fields chopping cotton. She worked in the fields by day, and by the light of a single coal-oil lamp at night, she did people's washing, ironing, and sewing.

When Callie worked in the fields, she'd put all the kids at the end of the row where she was working and have John, who was then six, watch them and keep them together.

A year passed and there was still no word from Ed. Callie knew he would be home soon, for he was never gone for much more than a year at a time.

After the cotton was laid by, there was no more work in the fields until the cotton was ready to be picked. Callie made do with what washing, ironing, and sewing she could do, plus, she had a small garden which provided them with fresh vegetables. When the wild berries and wild plums were in season, she picked all they could use. Black haws was another fruit they enjoyed in late summer. When times got lean, there were many days when Callie and the kids shared a single loaf of bread.

When the cotton bowls started to open, showing their snow-white blooms, Callie knew it would be only a few days until she could make money picking cotton. On the average, she could make from twenty to thirty cents per day picking cotton, but the cotton-picking time lasted for only a month. At least it would give her enough money for a couple of months.

The cold of winter caught Callie without work, and there was no food for the kids. The only thing they had to eat was a few dried beans they had raised the past summer, plus what walnuts and pecans they had gathered in the fall. They were running out fast. It had been a year and a half since Ed left, but Callie wouldn't give up. She knew that he would ride up just any day.

The food was now gone, and the kids were crying from hunger. Callie went to the store and tried to bargain for some supplies, saying that she would pay for them when Ed got home, but the storekeeper was not a charitable man. Afraid that Ed might not return, he would not extend her any credit. She finally managed to trade the only coal-oil lamp she had for a single sack of flour.

Callie made a deal with one of the neighbors to do some of their chores and milk their cow in exchange for some of the milk. That arrangement was working well, but then the flour ran out. She took the only piece of furniture she had and traded it for another sack of flour. The piece of furniture was Ed's rocking chair. No one was ever allowed to sit in Ed's rocker, not even the kids, and the only time Callie sat in it was to rock the baby to sleep. Actually, she did own one more thing—a stove which they used to cook with and to heat. The only bed was made out of an old door and a horsehair pad. The kids slept on the floor.

Hard winter was now on, and Ed still hadn't returned. The flour sack was near empty before Callie started getting work in.

As the warm air of spring started

flowing from the south, fields were made ready for planting and work would soon be aplenty. Callie knew now that they would make it through another season, and Ed would be home soon.

As spring advanced to summer, the early-morning sun caught Callie already in the field. It left her there as it faded below the horizon, giving way to the dark of night. Making their way home each night, Callie would sing to the kids. It made the journey shorter and kept harmony among the already well-mannered kids.

It had been two years since Ed had left, and Callie found herself with an empty feeling, a feeling of sorrow. It was a feeling she had known only when each of her four children had died. Only now, it was for the most important thing in her life and the only love she had ever known. She feared Ed would never return.

In the fall when the cotton was ready to pick, John was eight and Leo was seven, and Callie let them pick cotton with her. Ethyl, now five, watched Thelma and Dick. John could only make around eight cents a day, and Leo did good to make a nickel, but a penny was a penny, and remembering what last winter had been like, Callie knew every penny was important.

Nearing the end of the harvest, just as darkness was overcoming the light, Callie was making her way home, singing to the kids. As they neared the house, standing on the porch against the foreground of the dark house and a lightly darkened sky was the outline of a man. Callie knew it was Ed. As she took the last few steps and sang the last notes of the song, her voice quivered and tears of joy rolled down her cheeks. Ed was home.

Seven

The Tornado

Callie didn't go back to the fields. Ed had brought home plenty of money. One of the first things Ed did was reclaim his rocking chair from the storekeeper, and with a stern voice, expressed his displeasure with the way the storekeeper had dealt with Callie.

Ed moved Callie and the kids from Waco to Houston, where they bought a nice home just outside of town. It was the nicest place they had ever lived. He wanted Callie and the kids to live in luxury for a change.

In the spring, Ed had to leave, and Callie was with child again, but before he left, he bought Callie plenty of supplies and gave her enough money to get by until his return. Callie was afraid of losing the money, so she hid it under some boards in a can in the attic.

One spring day while she was working the garden, the sky started getting black, lightning started flashing, and the thunder began to rumble. The wind picked up and was blowing hard from the south. With every passing minute, the storm grew worse. Callie got the kids together, and they made their way to the cellar and waited out the storm. The storm raged on through the evening and into the night before silence began to muffle the sounds of distant thunder.

When Callie opened the door to the cellar, it was pitch black. Realizing that they couldn't see to make their way back to the house, she decided to spend the night in the cellar.

Early the next morning, just as the first rays of light made their way through the cracks in the cellar door,

Callie opened it and looked out. Beads of cold sweat popped from her skin and her heart throbbed as tears came to her eyes. The house was gone. There was nothing left, not even a single board.

While Ethyl watched Thelma and Dick, Callie took John and Leo and searched for miles, trying to find the small can containing the money she had hidden in the attic. They searched all day, but found nothing. They had lost everything they owned.

Callie was a strong woman, and without hesitation, she went to town, found a place to live, and took in washing, ironing, and sewing again.

Ed returned in late fall. Shortly after, Callie gave birth to a baby girl. She called her Lillian. Ed took Callie and the kids and moved to Sherman, Texas. Shortly after settling on a small farm just outside of town, Ed had to leave again. This time he didn't leave

Callie much money; he didn't have much to leave, but he told her that he would be back soon.

It wasn't long before their few supplies ran out, and with no money, once again, Callie moved into town and took in washing, ironing, and sewing.

Now with six kids and wanting them to be able to read and write, it was all Callie could do to keep the older ones in school and enough food on the table. She was a good mother and loved her children more than anything in the world. Even though she worked every waking hour, she always found time to play with the kids. The games they played were games they made up. Even though they were very competitive, there were never any losers. Callie believed in strong family ties and knew that love and togetherness strengthened those bonds.

Callie took the kids on a picnic at least once every week. The picnics were never more than a few yards from the house, but a picnic was a picnic, and no matter where they were, the picnics were always a lot of fun.

The days since Ed left turned into weeks, and the weeks turned into months. Then a year had gone by, but Callie knew that just any day now, Ed would ride up.

One hot afternoon, after almost two years, Ed found Callie and the kids working hard in the fields making ready for winter. His return sparked a short reign of happiness for Callie and the children, but it would last only as long as he was home.

Shortly after returning home, Ed moved Callie and the kids to the small town of Big Spring, Texas. He found a small place a few miles from town where they settled in. There were less than a hundred people in Big Spring, and it was eighty miles to the nearest town.

In the spring of 1897, with Callie three-months pregnant, Ed left home again. He swore to Callie that he wouldn't be gone long, but she had heard that before. She knew in her heart he'd be gone for a long time, but she also knew that he'd be back.

As spring slipped into summer, Callie and the kids made and worked a large garden, trying to grow enough food to feed everyone.

Big Spring was a small town. There was no farming done there, and in a town that small, there was no washing or sewing for Callie to do. All she could do was hope for Ed's early return. He had left her what little money he had, but it wasn't much.

As summer faded to fall, and fall gave way to winter, Ed had not returned. In the early part of winter, Callie gave birth to another girl. She named her Odessa.

By late winter the money was gone, as were the supplies and food they had raised from the garden the past summer, and there was still no sign of Ed.

Eight

The Early-Morning Fire

One morning while Callie was cooking breakfast, she started smelling smoke. At first she thought it was coming from the stove, but as the smell grew stronger, she decided there must be a range fire.

Since their breakfast was ready, she sat the food over to the side of the stove and ran outside to see which direction the fire was coming from. She discovered that the roof of their house was on fire!

She ran back into the house and hurried the children outside a safe distance away. She rushed in and out several times, trying to get all their belongings. Each time, the house was more engulfed in flames.

The last trip in, Callie was trying to make it to the stove where their breakfast was waiting, but the smoke was so heavy that she couldn't keep her eyes open. The heat was so intense that she had to hold her head down and cover her face with her arms.

Finally, realizing that she couldn't make it to the stove, she turned and headed for the front door. But only a step away from the door and safety, part of the ceiling gave way, knocking her to the floor.

The sudden jolt from the fall knocked the breath out of Callie. She lay there gasping for air. She felt the flesh on the back of her legs sizzling from the heat of the burning timbers. When she got her breath back, she screamed for help! She struggled and fought, trying to reach the door.

John and Leo were trying to get inside to help their mother, but the smoke and heat were so intense they couldn't make it through the door. They could hear her screams and knew she was just inside.

On what they knew would have to be their very last try, they were forced back by the intense heat. Leo had turned away, when John saw Callie's hand clawing at the sill of the front door. He grabbed her arm and began to pull. Then Leo found the other one. Both boys pulled with all their might. Callie was screaming shrill screams of fear and pain. Then, with one more hard pull, she was pulled free from the burning timbers. She fell to the ground with her dress ablaze!

While Leo was pulling his mother farther away from the fiery inferno, John began throwing dirt on her dress in an attempt to put out the fire. Once a safe distance from the burning house, Leo let go of his mother and helped John put out the fire on her clothes.

Callie's long, jet-black hair was now scorched to a dark brown, and it was not more than two inches long. Her arms were red and blistered from the intense heat, and the backs of her legs were cooked.

Her lungs were filled with smoke. She was coughing and heaving, trying to get air into them.

John, Leo, and the other kids, not knowing what to do, started patting her on the back, saying over and over, "It's okay now, Mama. You're going to be all right."

Callie struggled for life for a good hour. She was finally able to breathe without choking. It would be weeks before she would be able to talk normally.

The early-morning fire had failed to raise any neighbors because the fire had happened before anyone was out and about, and the nearest neighbor was two miles away. The fire hadn't lasted long, for the house was small and the wood was dry. One hour after the fire started, there was nothing left but a pile of smoking ashes.

Callie had managed to save all their belongings, but now they had no place to live. It was mid-afternoon before she was strong enough to put on the only other dress she owned.

Ethyl was now nine, and John was near twelve. Leo, coming up on eleven had to take over caring for the other children.

There were no other buildings on the farm, so all the kids except Lillian and Odessa started gathering grass and piling it around the tree where Callie lay so they would have a soft place to rest.

Late that afternoon Callie told John and Ethyl to fix supper. She talked them through it step by step.

Callie tried to eat, but her throat was so sore she couldn't swallow. She managed to get down only a few bites.

When it was all said and done, everyone was fed. It wasn't as good as Callie's cooking, but no one went hungry that night.

The low, dim glow of the morning's first light saw fourteen little eyes fully open and anxiously awaiting its arrival. To all, except Callie, it was fun camping out under the stars. John and Leo, being older, also enjoyed the change, but they knew that heartaches and hardships would soon overshadow and make short life of what fun they were having.

The sky was now in full light from the sun as it slowly rose above the brow of darkness. Callie was still unable to move about, so she talked the kids through cooking breakfast.

Callie was able to eat a little more that morning, but she was unable to eat a full meal. She was still nursing Odessa, and she knew that if she didn't get her strength back fast, there would be no food for the baby.

Ole Bess, their cow, had disappeared after the fire and hadn't come back. After breakfast, Callie had John and Leo search for her. She knew that without milk from the cow they would have it rough, and Odessa could not live, for she was now only six months old. John and Leo searched for Ole Bess all day. The sun was laying low in the sky when they returned empty-handed.

All the kids were crying from hunger. They hadn't eaten since breakfast. John and Leo helped Ethyl finish supper. Odessa was crying frantically from hunger. Callie tried nursing her, but after what she had been through, there wasn't enough milk to keep her alive for long.

After the beans were through cooking and the cornbread was fried, the kids ate their fill. With full stomachs once again, they were playing and having fun. Callie mashed some beans up real smooth and mixed them with a lot of juice and fed it to Odessa. It wasn't the best thing for her, but today it was all she would get.

As darkness started to fill the plains, Callie had all the kids to bed down near her, and she began telling them stories. Callie's way with stories made them all giggle and laugh. Her stories were for all ages. Her voice was rough and coarse, and her throat was in pain as she whispered to them until they all fell asleep.

The next morning after the moon had slipped below the western horizon and a good while before the sun would start nipping away at the darkness, there was a sound of brush rattling nearby. Callie and John woke instantly.

John whispered, "Mama, what's that?"

Callie replied, "Shhh," real low, then, "Listen."

There was more brush rattling— then the sound of a footstep. John sat up and moved close to Callie. He said, "I'm scared, Mama."

Callie reached out and touched John and said, "Shhh! It'll be all right." She gently squeezed his arm, giving him the reassurance he needed.

They both sat there for a long time, staring into the dark of a black moonless night. A few minutes passed and then footsteps. They seemed to be coming straight toward them. The brush started rattling—whoever or whatever it was was no more than a few feet away. Callie and John sat there, both scared to death, staring into the darkness, terrified!

There were no more sounds, but they knew that whatever was there was still there, and neither could close their eyes or turn their heads away.

It seemed like hours had passed before the first dim glow of light started eating at the dark black night. Slowly but surely the light overtook the darkness as it does every day. The first thing they saw was the faint outline of a giant creature. At least, that's what it looked like to Callie and John. The faded rough outline gradually began to take shape. John thought it was a bear, while Callie hoped it was Ed. As they continued to stare at the shape, there came a soft "Moooo." It was Ole Bess! She had come home!

John, recognizing the familiar sound, jumped to his feet! He ran and grabbed Bess around the neck, slapped her on the side real hard, and said, "You ole fool! You liked to have scared Mama and me to death!"

Ole Bess just licked John's arm with her sandpaper tongue, wanting salt. John jerked his arm away and said, "I'll get even with you for scaring me that way."

John sat back down near Callie, while all the other kids who were awakened by the noise were laughing and giggling. But John never did laugh about that deal, and he never forgot it, either. Callie told the story many times over the years, and it brought a lot of laughs to those who heard it.

Ole Bess's udder was full of milk, so John drew some water from the well, then rinsed out the milk pail and milked her. She hadn't been milked for two days so there would be plenty of milk today.

Callie was getting around better now and was trying to figure out what to do. In Big Spring there was no field work. There was no washing or ironing to be done. She knew she couldn't leave Big Spring, for if she did and Ed returned, he would never find her.

The nearest town was almost a hundred miles away. Callie knew they had survived tough times before, and they would survive this. They continued working the garden and gathering wild fruits and nuts.

As the weeks passed and the days grew shorter, and with their growing season coming to an end, Callie began worrying again. She knew as she felt the ever-increasing chill in the night air that they couldn't survive the winter under the shelter of a tree.

Nine

A Pocketful of Beans

Callie, now healed from the burns and with her hair growing back, took all the kids and went to the nearest neighbor. She told them of their tragedy.

The neighbors were sympathetic, but had no place for Callie and the kids to stay. They told her of an old abandoned shack about five miles away that might do for them to live in. They told her how to get there.

Callie took the kids and set out in search of the abandoned shack. It was still early afternoon when she found it. It was run down but liveable. There was a spring nearby which would provide plenty of water and just to the north of the shack was a gorge which would offer protection for Bess from the winter cold.

Callie and the kids headed home, figuring on moving the next day. By the time they got home, it was late and all the kids were hungry. Callie cooked supper while John milked Bess.

The next morning they gathered up all they could carry and headed for the shack which was to be their new home. It took several trips and several days, but it was finally done. It was none too soon, either, for cold weather was starting to set in.

John, Callie, and Leo took small twigs and made a thick mud. They used the mud and twigs, along with some grass, to chink the holes in the shack to keep out as much of the cold wind as possible.

Callie's hair was growing out and again had that lustrous shine that sparkled in the sunlight. She was getting around fine, and the deep burns on the backs of her legs were healing rapidly.

Winter came early that year. It caught them off-guard and unprepared.

Every day brought forth the same job—trying to keep warm. John and Leo spent most of each day gathering up dried cow chips and what dry twigs and sticks they could find. There were no trees to speak of around Big Spring and that made wood a scarce commodity.

The supplies were running out. The flour was gone, and there was no money. All that was left was a few pounds of dried beans. Each year it took more supplies to make it through the winter. There was usually an additional mouth to feed, and everyone was bigger and older. And the bigger they got, the more they ate.

The weather finally broke. Callie took all the kids and walked to town, a good four miles away. Once there, she asked about work. The answer was just about what she had expected in Big Spring—there was no work.

Callie and the kids went back

home. Every step of the way she worried about what they were going to do. Ole Bess was dry, so there was no milk, and there were no fruits, nuts, nor berries. There were only enough beans to last for three more days.

Callie rationed the beans and made them last for five days, believing every day that Ed would be home before they ran out. On the fifth day, she knew they were facing certain starvation.

There was a cold wind blowing out of the north. Odessa was now a year old, and Callie knew she couldn't carry her any distance in the freezing wind. And Lillian, now only four, couldn't walk very far. So she did the only thing she could think to do. She left all the kids with John, who was now thirteen, to watch, and she headed to town in the freezing cold.

Not having eaten anything to speak of for several days, because she wanted to stretch the food supply and make sure the kids got enough to eat, Callie had a hard time trying to keep up a brisk pace. She knew she would have to walk fast to keep warm. She found herself getting weak and out of breath, but she knew she had to go on. It was the love for her children that continued pulling at her inner strength, allowing her to take one more step and then one more.

The winter storm was turning into what was to be the worst storm of the winter. The temperature was still falling, and the wind was blowing harder. Callie leaned farther into the wind. Her body was now near a forty-five-degree angle to the ground. Holding her head down to keep her face covered with her folded arms, she glanced up from time to time, hoping to see the few buildings that made up the town of Big Spring.

Now weak and barely able to walk, Callie glanced up again. She saw no buildings. She hesitated, having reached the point of giving up. But then, she thought about the seven children back at the cabin who would certainly starve to death or freeze if she didn't get back, and somehow from somewhere she got the strength to take another step and then another.

Time and motion had now lost all meaning to Callie. All she could think of was one more step. Then, as she glanced up into the north wind, she made out the outlines of buildings which made up Big Spring. She let out a sigh of relief as she found another surge of inner strength— enough to carry her the rest of the way to the Big Spring General Store.

Once inside, Callie sat down on a keg near the pot-bellied stove, trying to warm her frozen body. She sat there for almost an hour before she was able to talk to the store owner.

Finally, she stood up and walked over to the counter. She looked at the owner and said, "My husband is away somewhere working for Wells Fargo. Our house burned a while back, and my seven children and I have nothing to eat. We are completely out of supplies, and we have no money. I'd like to get some supplies on credit until my husband returns."

The store owner replied, "Sorry, lady. It's all I can do just to keep the store open, and there's simply no way I can let anyone have credit."

Callie pleaded and tried to bargain with the man, but it was no use. He wouldn't give an inch. She was now in a panic. Her heart was racing, and her mind was going a hundred miles an hour. She had to do something, but what?

Just then a man walked into the store, and as the store owner turned to greet him, Callie, thinking only about the survival of her children, began filling her pockets with dried beans from an open sack sitting on the floor next to her. The store owner turned just in time to see her putting the last handful in her pocket.

He yelled, "Hey! What do you think you're doing?" as he headed for Callie.

She tried to get around him and run out of the store, but he caught her. She had only enough beans in her pocket to feed her family for one day. All she had thought about was keeping them from starving.

The store owner said to the other man, "Quick, Bill! Go get the marshal!"

"There's no need for that," the man replied. "What she took doesn't cost more than five cents."

The store owner yelled, "It doesn't matter how much or how little it cost! We don't want thieves in Big Spring!"

The man argued in Callie's behalf, and after a time the store owner agreed to let him pay for the beans and forget about the incident.

The man offered to give Callie a

ride home and, remembering how cold it was and how near frozen she was when she had reached town, she accepted.

The man, who was a stranger to Callie, loaded his supplies onto his wagon and then helped her on board. On the way home he asked her a million questions, seemingly wanting to know all about her.

Callie told him about Ed and all the kids, then said, "I expect Ed home just any day."

As they neared Callie's cabin, he pointed toward the east and told her, "My ranch house is that way. It's only a mile from here."

When they reached the cabin, Callie got down and thanked him for all he had done. He said, "Don't mention it. It was my pleasure," then drove off toward the east.

Callie went inside and warmed herself by the fire. She knew the beans she had in her pocket would only feed them one more day. She just knew that Ed would be home the next day.

By the next morning the wind had laid somewhat. Callie was cooking all the food they had. By late evening, fully realizing that this would be their last meal, she looked at the beans in the pot and thought, "I'll ration these beans and make them last for two or, hopefully, three days." She fed the children, but she herself did not eat.

The next day she took what was left and divided it in half and fed the kids. Again, she did not eat.

The children were crying from hunger. Odessa and Lillian were crying frantically from stomach pains. Callie had never been in a church, but she knew there was a God. That night as the children lay nestled close to each other on the quilt on the floor, she knelt on the floor and prayed.

Ten

"Meet Me in the Gorge"

The next morning brought a gray sky and a cold north wind. Callie was very weak. Odessa was crying, and Lillian's eyes were sunken back in her head. The beans on the stove were barely enough for one person, but today they would feed seven.

It was late afternoon before Callie fed the children what was left. They all cried for more, but there was no more. Callie again didn't eat. It had been four days since she had eaten, and she knew she couldn't last much longer.

The next day brought nothing but bitter cold. The children were weak and lifeless, and hope was fading fast. Callie knew the children were slowly dying, but there was nothing she could do. The day was long, and the cabin was filled with moans and cries of starving children.

The next day brought more of the same. It was almost noon when the stranger who had helped Callie out of trouble and given her a ride home pulled up in front of the cabin. He had with him a sack of flour, a sack of beans, a sack of sugar, and a cured pork shoulder. He carried the supplies inside.

The man noticed that the children were in bad shape, and the younger ones were near death. This time he introduced himself. His name was Bill Wilson.

Callie mixed up some sugar water and fed it to the children. This would give them energy and help build up their strength. Bill had Callie drink a big glass, too. The children responded to the sugar water very fast, as did Callie.

Bill helped Callie make a big pan of biscuits, and then they fried some ham.

They also put on a big pot of beans. It would take the beans several hours to cook, but the biscuits and ham would hold them until the beans were done.

Callie fed the children well for the next few days. They were building their strength back fast.

The weather was much nicer now that the winter storm had broken. All the kids were acting normal, and Callie was feeling better.

Nearly a week had gone by when Bill Wilson stopped by again. He told Callie that he had just stopped by to check on them.

When Bill got ready to leave, Callie walked with him to the wagon. As he climbed up and sat down, he looked down at her and said, "There's plenty more where that came from, if you know what I mean."

With a puzzled look on her face, Callie replied, "I'm sorry. I don't understand."

Bill said, "Let me put it this way. If you don't want your kids to go hungry, meet me this evening just after sundown in the gorge just east of here."

Fully understanding the implications of Bill's statement, she turned and rushed back into the cabin. Her heart was racing and she was shaking all over as she turned and locked the door.

After a time she settled down and started cooking the children some supper. Her mind kept drifting back to what Bill had said, and each time she got more nervous and scared.

That evening, as the sun inched ever so close to the horizon, Callie could think of nothing else but what to do. As the reddish glow of the western sky faded to a darkened gray—held only from total darkness by a half moon which was straight overhead, she realized full well that if she didn't visit the gorge they would all die of hunger. Reluctantly, she told John, "Watch the kids. I'll be back in a little while." With a heavy heart, she walked out the door and headed for the gorge.

For the rest of the winter and through early spring they never ran out of food, but each time supplies were brought to the cabin, Callie made another trip to the gorge.

Ed had been gone for nigh on two and a half years. Unknown to Callie, he had joined the army to fight in the Spanish American War. He had been seriously wounded in the charge up San Juan Hill and was lying in a hospital somewhere in Georgia. He was paralyzed, and the doctors didn't hold much hope for his recovery.

There was no way of letting Callie know and, even if there were, he didn't want her to know, because he didn't want to be a burden to her. So she went on believing that he would ride up before sundown. She believed that every day.

In early May Bess freshened, so there was plenty of milk. The greens in the garden were ready and soon the berries would be ripe. Once again food would be aplenty. Callie made a vow that she would never make another trip to the gorge.

Wanting to keep that vow and insure their survival that summer and, if necessary, winter, Callie and the children raised four times as much garden as they ever had before.

The warm summer brought good health to all. The kids didn't seem to mind as much this year having to work in the garden. They could all remember their narrow escape from death last winter.

Fall found the entire family in the garden harvesting the crop they had nurtured. Dried beans and peas were aplenty. There was no way they would run out of those. And they had more corn than they could possibly use. The corn they carried a little at a time to the mill in Big Spring, where it was ground into corn-meal on shares.

The owner of the mill had a small .22 rifle that John admired very much. After several convincing arguments with Callie, she finally agreed to try and trade some corn and beans for the rifle and some shells. It took a lot of dickering back and forth, but she finally managed to trade for the .22 rifle and two boxes of bullets.

Callie told John to take five bullets to practice with and then be sure to make every one count. John spent a lot of time just lying on the ground looking down the barrel of his new rifle, sighting in on a target. It took all day for him to use all five practice shots.

Early the next morning John was ready for the real thing. Callie watched as he left the cabin and headed toward brushy country. She thought to herself what a handsome boy he was. He was now fifteen and rapidly growing into manhood. She had noticed more and more every day how much like Ed he was.

John was back at the cabin by noon. He had fired two shots and had two rabbits. He became quite good with the little rifle, very seldom missing a shot. He was keeping meat on the table.

After about a week he decided to try for a deer. He always saw plenty of them every time he went hunting, but he hadn't wanted to waste a bullet trying to bring one down. But now he had a plan. He figured he would stalk the deer until he had a sure shot at the heart or dead smack between the eyes.

He headed for a spot he knew where the brush stopped at the edge of a small ravine. There was nothing but wide open plains beyond that point. The ravine would allow him to move up and down the edge of the open plain, while the brush would offer concealment while he watched for a sure shot. He also knew that if the wind was calm or blowing in his face he would stand a better chance of getting a deer.

He walked along the upper side of the ravine just keeping in the edge of the brush where he could see the plains. It was noon before he spotted a herd of deer. They were still a good ways down from where he was. He could see the young ones running and playing. He felt a slight breeze against his face and knew they couldn't smell him. He decided to slip down into the ravine and move closer to the herd.

John moved down the ravine to a point where he thought he should be straight in front of the deer. As he made his way out of the ravine and crawled to the edge of the clearing, he saw them just a short distance away. He decided to wait and see if they would move closer. He lay there for a long time, but they didn't seem to be drifting in any certain direction. He lay still for another hour. Finally they started wandering his way.

They were not more than fifty yards away now, but John was afraid to shoot from that distance. He didn't think he could get one with it that far away. Then, slowly the deer moved closer. Now they were only twenty yards away, and John thought, "It's now or never." He took a fine bead on a big buck, aiming right for the heart.

As the shot rang out, the deer jumped straight up, then fell to the ground. It started kicking, trying to get up. Once on his feet, he took off like a flash through the brush, right behind the others.

John knew he had hit the deer and hoped he'd be able to track it down. He soon found drops of blood and knew he had found the trail. He followed the trail, being as quiet as possible. He figured the deer would run a ways and then lie down.

He tracked the deer for a good hour being ever so careful, watching his every step, trying not to make any noise at all. Then his eye caught a glimpse of the dark gray of the deer's winter coat.

He froze. Then he knelt to the ground and listened. He could hear no sounds at all. He crept ever so slowly toward what he thought was the deer. He had to be careful not to brush against any of the brush and not step on any twigs. He knew that the slightest noise would scatter the already frightened herd.

John, now growing nervous, paused for a few minutes to calm down. As he advanced closer, the dark gray hair started to take form. It was the deer. It was lying flat on its side. None of the others were around.

The deer lying flat on its side was a sure sign that it was dead. And sure 'nuf, as he stood up and looked closely at the big buck, he saw that it was dead. Now very proud, he hoisted it around his neck and headed for the cabin. It was quite heavy. He had to stop and rest several times along the way. When he finally reached the cabin, everyone cheered and rejoiced. The Nicholson family would never go hungry again.

Winter was well on its way out, and Ed had been gone for three years. There was still plenty of beans, peas, and corn, so Callie, knowing they had plenty to spare, took some to town and traded for clothes for everyone.

The store owner was nice to Callie and seemed to have forgotten the incident of the year before. As she and the children got ready to leave the store, the owner said, "I've got a half dozen chickens that someone traded me, and I have no use for them. You can have them if you want them."

"Thank you. That's very nice of you," Callie replied.

John and Leo gathered up the chickens, and they headed home. The two boys set in building a chicken coop just a short ways from the house. They used branches from some of the larger brush for ribs and wove smaller branches to form panels. The panels were tied together to form the coop. They made nests for the chickens from dead, dry grass.

They were now getting five eggs every day. One of the chickens was a rooster. These were the first eggs they'd had in three years.

Three and a half years had passed since Ed had left, but Callie wouldn't give up hope. She told the kids every day that their daddy would be back just any day. But she didn't know the awful truth.

Eleven

A Fast Train to Texas

The doctors had seen no improvement in Ed's condition and had told him that he would most likely be paralyzed for the rest of his life. They wanted to send him home to be with Callie, but he wouldn't hear of it. Even though he loved her, he wouldn't let himself be a burden to her.

Then one day in late summer of 1899, the doctors noticed a slight improvement in Ed's condition. It wasn't enough to warrant any additional hope for his recovery, but it did cause them to put him on an intense therapy program.

Back in Texas one of the neighbors offered John a job working on his ranch. John knew he couldn't leave home because everyone had come to depend on him, but he also knew how much a little money would mean. He finally struck a deal with the rancher. He agreed to work for him for a year in exchange for a horse, a saddle, and a side arm. He also told the rancher that the next spring he wanted a plow and the use of a horse to plow and keep up their garden.

The rancher agreed to give them a plow and loan them a horse. This meant that Leo would have to take over most of the responsibilities at home.

When Leo agreed to take care of things, John started riding the range. He spent most of his time herding the cows to where the best grazing was. There was no such thing as a day off or going home at night. He saw the family about once a month, and then it was for only a short time. That winter turned out to be a long, cold winter for John. He spent most of it outside. Most of the nights were spent there as well.

As spring started to break, John talked to the rancher about the plow. A couple of days later the rancher took John into town with the buckboard, leading a workhorse in harness. They stopped by the general store and picked up a new double shovel and delivered it to the cabin for Leo. They arrived there just after noon, and Callie insisted that they stay for an early supper. The rancher agreed, so Callie set in on fixing supper.

Leo had killed a couple of prairie chickens, and Callie had them already boiled. She also had a pot of beans left from the day before. She made up a batch of egg noodles to cook in with the prairie chickens, and she made a big skillet of gravy to go with the light bread that she made twice a week. It was a meal that the rancher would not soon forget, and John would think about it many times while he was on the range eating hardtack.

Time was passing, and the children

were growing up. The four years Ed had been gone soon turned into four and a half. His condition was improving slowly. He was now able to move his arms and legs but wasn't able to get out of bed on his own. Callie still looked for him to ride up every day.

The four and a half years soon turned into five. Ed was now able to get up, and with the aid of his crutches could get around. He would still not go home. He would not be a burden to the ones he loved.

Things were a lot easier for Callie and the children now. John was bringing home money, not much, but it was a lot more than they were used to. Leo had taken on the responsibility for the garden and chores.

Ole Bess had had a heifer calf two years before and now there were two cows to milk. That meant milk aplenty. At times when the grass was lush and green, there was more milk than they could use.

It was spring, 1902. Odessa, the youngest, was now four and a half years old. Things were much easier on Callie now. It had been five years since Ed had left, but she still insisted that he'd be home any day.

John was now seventeen and was still working on a ranch. Leo, now sixteen, had taken a shine to a young girl in town. She had a twin sister, and he had a little trouble telling them apart. He didn't get to see her very often, but he made it to town as often as he could.

Odessa turned five. She was Mama's little helper. Ethyl, Thelma, Dick, and Lillian were all growing up, too.

For the next few months very little changed from day to day for Callie, but things were starting to happen for Ed. By the end of summer he was able to get around without his crutches. He started feeling like a whole man again and found himself wanting to go home. He was now forty-one years old, and Callie was thirty-four.

Ed's condition was now improving very rapidly, and, by the middle of winter, he was able to do just about anything. In late January after almost six years, he caught the train and headed toward Texas.

On the way to Texas Ed recalled that he had met Callie twenty-three years ago, and at that time there were very few railroad tracks. It seemed that now they were everywhere, connecting all the small towns together like wagon trails used to do. He also noted that telegraph lines ran the full length of every track, and every railway station had a telegraph office. The old Butterfield stage lines and Wells Fargo stage had been replaced by the steam engine.

Ed saw a steam engine on wheels that didn't need a track to travel on and wondered if that was the wave of the future.

The railroad brought fast, comfortable travel, but it was leaving behind a way of life that soon would be forgotten. Ed wondered if a man could really be happy living in such a fast-paced world.

As the train stopped at every little town, they unloaded freight and mail. Passengers got off and passengers got on. Even with all these stops, it would take a good horse ten days to cover the same ground the train could cover in one.

After nearly six days on the train, Ed got off in a town called San Angelo. He was still seventy miles from Big Spring, but there was no railroad to Big Spring yet. He would have to buy a horse and ride the rest of the way.

Ed had always been partial to buckskin horses. He found a good one at the livery. The livery owner priced the horse and saddle at sixty dollars.

Ed, thinking that was the best deal he had run across in awhile, didn't fuss about the price. He just paid the livery owner the sixty dollars.

Ed had seen horses of this caliber with saddle and all sell for a good two hundred dollars plus. Why, even he had paid as much as a hundred and fifty dollars and that was without the saddle. What he didn't know was that prices were down. He could have bought a good horse for as little as twenty dollars, and a good saddle wouldn't have cost more than five.

Ed stopped by the general store and picked up a few supplies before heading out. He figured on a good two-day ride and got only enough to last that long. He noted that a lot of food was in cans and ready to eat. All you had to do was open the can. He'd seen a little of it in the past but not much.

Having got his supplies, he rolled a cigarette, mounted up, and headed home.

It was early afternoon when he

headed out. He spent the first night camped along the river. That was the first night he'd slept under the stars in a long time.

Twelve

The Homecoming

The next morning found Ed on the trail at first light, eating breakfast out of a can. He found himself anxious to get home.

As the sun drifted below the horizon, he was still a few miles from home, so he made camp again. That night he couldn't sleep. It had been almost six years since he had seen his family. Were they still alive? Were they dead? He had refused to send word that he was hurt, but alive, and of course, there had been no word from them.

Sometime before morning he fell asleep only to be awakened a short time later by the nickering of his horse. He opened his eyes and saw a faint light in the eastern sky. The sun was coming up.

It was now the first of February. It wasn't just real cold, but it was still quite chilly. He got up and rolled up his bedroll. The thought of seeing Callie and the children again caused his pulse to quicken. He wondered if Callie was still as beautiful as ever, and if she would forgive him for not letting her know that he was alive. Suddenly, a terrible thought hit him! "What if Callie has remarried? What if she believed I was dead and married someone else? She'd need help raising the children."

He threw the saddle on his horse and tightened the girth. He turned, remembering the campfire and quickly stamped it out. He scattered the smoldering embers, then took his canteen and poured water on them. They hissed, smoked, and went out. He jumped in the saddle, slapped the horse with the reins, and took off at a gallop.

It was late morning when Ed arrived at the place where he had left Callie and the kids six years ago. He pulled the horse up short, then sat perfectly still, staring at the spot where the house had stood. It was gone.

He knew the house had burned a long time back, but nature had reclaimed the spot where it stood. There were large dried-up weeds and grass, and even young brush growing there. It, though, was dormant—like all the rest—waiting for the warmth of spring to start another growing season.

Ed headed for town, figuring on finding out where his family might be. As he rode into Big Spring, he figured that if anyone knew anything about them, it would be, the General Store. He walked inside and asked the store owner if he knew of Callie and the children. He was told where they were living. He mounted up and headed back south.

On the way, in Ed had ridden within a quarter of a mile of where they were living and didn't know it. It was only four miles to the cabin, but he figured it to be the longest four miles he had ever ridden.

It was mid-afternoon when the cabin came into full view. As the cabin got closer, his heart started to pound— lightly at first, but with every step the horse took, the pounding grew harder and faster.

About a quarter of a mile away, Leo saw a rider coming. When he reached the porch, he stopped and watched the rider approach. He was just ten years old the last time he saw his dad, but when he saw the big hat and the two ivory-handled pistols, he knew who the stranger was. He turned toward the house and yelled, "Mama! Hey, Mama! Dad's home!"

Callie flew out the door, then paused on the steps as Ed pulled up his horse and dismounted. Leo took the horse and tied the reins to a nearby bush.

Callie and Ed stood there just staring at each other. Then, as Ed started raising his arms, Callie leaped from the porch, never touching the ground, and landed in his arms, where they embraced in silence for a long time. It would have lasted longer, but all the children were pulling and hollering at their daddy.

Ed released Callie, then bent down and picked up Odessa and asked, "Who's this?"

"This is the one you've never seen. Her name is Odessa," Callie answered.

Odessa looked into her daddy's eyes and asked, "Do you want me for your little girl?"

Ed smiled and said, "I shore do!" then hugged her tightly.

Leo took Ed's horse and rode to find John to tell him that their Dad had come home.

Ed had been gone for six years. All the other times that he'd been gone for so many months at a time, Callie had never once asked him where he'd been or what he'd been doing. But this time it had been six years, and she had to know.

That night, after all the kids were asleep, she poured two cups of coffee and carried them over to the small table that stood beside the chair Ed was sitting in. They didn't have enough furniture, so she sat on the floor beside him.

She waited until he had finished about half of his coffee, then she took a deep breath and said, "Ed, I've never interfered with your job. I've never asked you where you've been. But Ed, it's been six years! You've been gone for six long, hard years! There's been a few times when I've wanted to just give up and die. Where have you been, Ed? What's kept you away for so long?"

In the glow of the lamplight, Ed

looked down at Callie with such love and admiration in his eyes that the bad memories of those six years took wings and they flew right out of her heart. Suddenly it felt light.

He reached out and placed his once-paralyzed hand on her head. He stroked her shiny black hair and said, "When the Spanish American War broke out, I joined up. I rode with Teddy Roosevelt in the charge up San Juan Hill. I was wounded pretty bad. I was paralyzed and thought I'd never walk again. I just couldn't come home a cripple. It was only after I started to get feeling back in my legs that I began to have hope. Finally, I was able to walk. Then, I tried to ride. I fell off a few times, but one day I stayed on. It was then that I knew it was time to come home."

Callie laid her head on Ed's knee. She was trying to absorb all that he had told her. Tears came to her eyes, then ran down her cheeks and fell on the faded cotton dress she was wearing. She was picturing him lying there paralyzed. She was feeling his pain, and remembering her own. There had been times when she'd doubted he would ever come home.

Ed squeezed Callie's shoulder and said, "One of the happiest days of my life was the day I could ride a horse again and realized I could come home."

He looked at Callie's upturned face and added, "I shore do love you, Callie. I love the kids, too."

They sat there in the glow of the coal-oil lamp thinking about their lives together. There had been good times and bad times, but for Callie, the last couple of years, when she thought Ed was never coming home, were the worst years of all.

Ed said, "Callie, tell me what you and the kids have been doing. How did you make do? How did you feed and clothe them all?"

Callie began talking, and an hour later, she had filled Ed in on just about everything that had happened since he'd been gone.

All the years they had been married Callie had never asked Ed for anything, but that night she said, "Ed, take me away from this God-forsaken place!"

Ed agreed, and the next morning he rode into town and brought back a team and wagon full of supplies. When Leo saw his dad drive up in the wagon with two horses tied to the back, he got excited. Ed had brought home a horse, a pistol, and a rifle for Leo. John had just gotten there and was standing on the porch. Now the whole family was together again.

When Callie heard Ed drive up, she ran to the door. He climbed down out of the wagon, and she ran to meet him. He grabbed her hands and slung her around and said, "Callie, pack up! We're moving!"

They didn't have many belongings,

so the packing didn't take long. While everyone was loading up the wagon, John went to his boss and picked up what pay he had coming. When he got back, the Nicholson family headed out.

Thirteen

And the Waters Flow On

They had traveled for more than a week before stopping near a small town called Wichita Falls. They made camp a couple of miles from the Red River.

The next morning Ed went into town. That evening, when he came back to camp, he said, "Callie, I've bought us a house about a mile from town."

Callie's mouth dropped open. She asked, "Where's the money coming from, Ed?"

He said, "We needn't worry about money, Callie. I've got six years' back pay in my pocket."

They spent the next couple of weeks fixing up things around the new place. John and Leo worked on the barn

129

and corral, while the girls tidied up the house. This was the best house they had ever lived in.

After settling in, John found work at the livery stable, Leo got a job at the general store, and Ed went back to work with the Texas Rangers.

Ed had been home for three months when Callie told him she was again with child. The baby was born in 1904. It was a little girl. Callie named her Margie. When Margie was born, Ed was away on a manhunt. He didn't stay gone for very long at a time now. He was never gone for more than two months.

Margie was a year old when Callie told Ed she was pregnant again. This one was a boy, born on a cold winter night when Ed was in Dallas. Callie named him Ernest.

Eleven months later, at the age of thirty nine, Callie gave birth again—a son, stillborn. This time Ed was someplace in Oklahoma.

In late spring, one year later, Callie was once again going into labor. This time it was a girl. She was a duplicate of Callie. Her eyes were bright blue, her hair was jet black, and her skin was very light. Callie named her Callie.

Ed was somewhere in New Mexico when baby Callie was born. He returned when she was two weeks old.

In June of 1909, Leo came home one day with a beautiful girl. It was the same girl he had met in Big Spring. Her name was Virginia. She was teaching school in Wichita Falls. Her twin sister, Laura, taught school in Waco.

Virginia and Leo were married a week later. Since they both had good jobs, they bought a house in town.

In July of 1909, Ed brought home a little red wagon for the kids. Dick, Lillian, and Odessa took turns pulling Margie and Ernest around the yard. Everyone was having a good time. They were having the time of their lives. Then the little red wagon hit a small rock and turned over, throwing both Margie and Ernest against the foundation of the house. Both children started crying. They wanted no more of the wagon.

The next morning when Callie woke the children, Ernest wouldn't wake up. When she reached down to pick him up, she knew he was dead. They figured he had died from injuries caused when the wagon turned over.

Callie felt pain and sorrow, but she couldn't let it show, because all the other kids needed her.

One week after Ernest's death, baby Callie came down with a high fever. Callie did all she knew to do. Ed even sent for the doctor, but baby Callie died three days later from unknown causes.

Baby Callie's death cut deep into Callie's heart. Losing two children in two weeks was almost more than she could bear, and yet she knew she must be strong. From somewhere deep within, she drew the strength to go on. But in the dark of night, when all the kids were asleep, her strength would fade and tears of sorrow and the pain of grief would haunt her through the night.

One month after baby Callie's death, Ethyl got married to a man from Sherman, Texas. When she moved away, Thelma went with her. Ethyl's husband had gotten a job for Thelma working in the bank there in Sherman. Later, Thelma married the banker's son.

The year 1909 was now over. It had been a year that burned deep in Callie's heart and mind.

In June of 1911, Callie once again gave birth—a boy she named Jessie. Ed was in Sherman, Texas, when Jessie was born. He was visiting with Ethyl and Thelma.

July 28, 1914, was the beginning of

World War I. John joined the army just as soon as the war broke out. Leo was drafted sometime later.

Ed was fifty three when the war broke out. He tried to join up, but they said he was too old. They wouldn't take him. He had spent thirty-six years fighting for his country in one way or another. He had fought for law and order with the Texas Rangers from the time he was eighteen. He had hunted down train robbers, stagecoach robbers, and bank robbers for Wells Fargo. He had fought in the Spanish American War. And he was determined not to let this war pass him by.

There was a young general in Oklahoma City that Ed had served with in the Spanish American War. The young general was then a second lieutenant fresh out of West Point. In the Spanish American War, Ed was a captain, and the young lieutenant was in his command. Ed had taken a liking to the young lieutenant and had recommended him for the Distinguished Service Cross for Heroism.

Ed took Callie and the kids and moved to Oklahoma City, hoping to convince the young general to help him get into the war. He moved them to the small town of Washington, just north of Oklahoma City.

While Callie and the children were setting up house, Ed went to see the young general and managed to convince him to help him get into the war. The general approved a waiver on Ed's age and had him assigned to his unit with his former rank of captain.

Three months later, in late winter of 1915, at the age of fifty four, Ed shipped out for Europe.

In the summer of 1916, Callie got word that Leo had been wounded in action and had been sent home. He was hospitalized for a time, then after he was released from the hospital, he and Virginia went to Washington, Oklahoma, to visit Callie.

In June of 1917, while on an offensive, Ed's company came under heavy machine-gun fire. While trying to destroy the machine-gun nest, Ed was shot several times. He was given up for dead two different times, but he wasn't ready to die. He was eventually shipped to a hospital in Oklahoma City.

Ed spent the next two years in the hospital. He was first released in July, 1919. However, he was in and out of the hospital all the time.

On July 18, 1920, their sixteenth child was born. Callie named her Irene. Then on March 1, 1922, their last child was born—a boy named Jack. Callie was fifty three and Ed was sixty one.

It seemed that 1922 was a good year for marrying, for at age thirty six John finally married. Lillian and Odessa were also married that same year. Then, in the spring of 1923, at age nineteen, Margie married. Margie was a beautiful young lady and was envied by all who knew her.

Irene was Ed's favorite. She always called him Papa. He had never been around when the others were growing up, but he was always there for Irene.

Irene recalled that her papa always smoked a pipe. One day when she was about four years old, Ed went to town, and Callie was out back washing clothes. Irene was in the house alone. She got her papa's favorite pipe and packed it with tobacco, then lit it. She got very sick! She climbed down out of her chair and ran over to the fireplace and threw the pipe in it!

When Ed started looking for his pipe, he couldn't find it. He asked, "Has anyone seen my pipe?"

Everyone except Irene said, "No." Irene didn't say a word.

That night Ed picked up Irene and

kissed her on the cheek and asked, "Have you seen my pipe, honey?"

She replied, "Yes, Papa. I burned it."

"Why did you do that?" Ed asked.

"Well, Papa, I smoked it and it made me sick. I knew it would make you sick, too. I didn't want you to get sick, so I burned it," Irene replied.

Ed just laughed. If anyone else had touched his pipe, there would have been the devil to pay.

Ed was still in and out of the hospital all the time. He was operated on several times, and each time the recovery was longer and harder.

In 1926, during the hottest part of the summer, Margie, with child, had an attack of appendicitis and died before they could get her to a hospital. Callie once again felt the deep burning pain one feels from losing a part of themselves.

In late April, 1928, Ed was rushed to the hospital. He had been in a lot of pain for several days. The doctors operated on him, trying to save him, but he continued to get worse.

Callie spent every spare minute at the hospital with Ed. Their youngest child was six years old and in school, so Callie stayed with Ed during the day. She would sit beside his bed, remembering all the things they had been through together.

It had been forty-eight years since they had made their vows to each other under the stars on a gravel bar somewhere in Louisiana. And even though Ed had left Callie alone a lot, he had never once spoken in anger to her. He had always treated her like a queen.

The doctors did all they knew to do, but on May 4, 1928, Elischa George Nicholson died at the age of sixty eight. The cause of death was listed as complications from injuries received in World War I. He was buried with full military honors in Washington, Oklahoma.

In 1929 Callie moved for the last time. She and the three remaining children moved to Arkansas, to a small community called Cove Creek, eight miles south of the little town of Prairie Grove.

Two of the kids grew up and left home, but Dick never married. He lived with Callie. Then, in June of 1954, Dick died.

On December 4, 1956, two and a half years later, Callie Many Waters Cox Nicholson drew her last breath. I cried that day, for at age eighty seven, my Grandma Callie was dead.